SPOTLIGHT ON NATIVE AMERICANS

SIOUX

Lorraine Harrison

New York

Published in 2016 by The Rosen Publishing Group, Inc.
29 East 21st Street, New York, NY 10010

First Edition

Editor: Katie Kawa
Book Design: Samantha DeMartin
Reviewed by: Robert J. Conley, Former Sequoyah Distinguished Professor at Western Carolina University and Director of Native American Studies at Morningside College and Montana State University.
Supplemental material reviewed by: Donald A. Grinde, Jr., Professor of Transnational/American Studies at the State University of New York at Buffalo.

Photo Credits: Cover Wolfgang Kaehler/LightRocket/Getty Images; pp. 4–5 DEA Picture Library/ De Agostini Picture Library/Getty Images; p. 7 Wollertz/Shutterstock.com; p. 8 Lorraine Logan/ Shutterstock.com; p. 9 Robert Van Der Hilst/Gamma-Rapho/Getty Images; pp. 11 (Red Cloud), 12–13, 12 (inset), 14 courtesy of the Library of Congress; p. 11 (Crazy Horse) Telrúnya/Wikimedia Commons; p. 15 Walter Bibikow/The Image Bank/Getty Images; p. 16 National Register of Historic Places in the United States of America/Wikimedia Commons; pp. 17, 19 Marilyn Angel Wynn/Nativestock/Getty Images; pp. 20–21 John Coletti/Photolibrary/Getty Images; p. 22 Frederick M. Brown/Getty Images Entertainment/Getty Images; p. 23 John Sunderland/Denver Post/Getty Images; p. 24 AFP/AFP/ Getty Images; p. 25 Peter Davis/Archive Photos/Getty Images; p. 27 Jean-Marc Giboux/Hulton Archive/Getty Images; p. 29 Hyoung Chang/Denver Post/Getty Images.

Library of Congress Cataloging-in-Publication Data

Harrison, Lorraine, 1959- author.
   Sioux / Lorraine Harrison.
      pages cm. — (Spotlight on Native Americans)
   Includes index.
ISBN 978-1-5081-4160-0 (pbk.)
ISBN 978-1-5081-4161-7 (6 pack)
ISBN 978-1-5081-4163-1 (library binding)
1. Dakota Indians—History—Juvenile literature. I. Title.
E99.D1H26 2016
978.004'975243—dc23
                              2015027671

Manufactured in the United States of America

CPSIA Compliance Information: Batch #BW16PK: For Further Information contact Rosen Publishing, New York, New York at 1-800-237-9932

CONTENTS

WHO ARE THE SIOUX?
CHAPTER 1

The Sioux are one of the hundreds of Native American communities that live in the United States. They have their own **unique** history and **culture**. The Sioux people's way of life has always been influenced by the land around them. They live mainly in North Dakota, South Dakota, Minnesota, and Montana.

The Sioux are known for their many conflicts with the U.S. government. However, they're also known for their rich traditions, their love for the land, and their language. The Siouan language is spoken throughout North America, including by peoples that aren't called Sioux.

Depending on which of the three main **dialects** of the Siouan language they speak, Sioux people call themselves Lakotas (also called the Tetons), Naktoas (or Yanktons), or Dakotas (or Santees). These are the three main divisions of the Sioux nation.

The name "Sioux," however, didn't come from the Siouan language. Instead, it came from the language of the Ojibwe people, who were their neighbors. In the Ojibwe language, "Sioux" means "adders," which are a kind of poisonous snake. The Sioux don't easily back down from a fight, whether it's with their Ojibwe neighbors or with U.S. leaders.

Bison were very important to the Sioux people throughout their history. These animals once roamed the large areas of land where the Sioux lived.

BORN FROM THE BLACK HILLS

CHAPTER 2

Scientists and historians still don't know exactly how long ago the ancestors of Native Americans first traveled to North America. As such, the exact date of the arrival of the Sioux's ancestors in North America is unknown. However, like most Native American people, the Sioux have, for centuries, told an origin story that explains how they came to live here.

According to Sioux elders, the first Sioux came from Star Nation to a place beneath the earth. Then, they emerged from Wind Cave in the Black Hills of present-day South Dakota. The Sioux call the Black Hills *Paha Sapa*, which means "the heart of everything that is." That land is a sacred place for the Sioux people, as well as other communities of Plains Indians, such as the Cheyennes.

The Sioux once lived in what's now Minnesota, Wisconsin, Iowa, and Illinois. However, they began to move farther west after wars with the Ojibwe people. They also moved to follow the bison they hunted.

Today, the Sioux are one of the largest Native American nations. They're linked by their language, lifestyle, and shared history. It's believed there are well over 100,000 people of Sioux **descent** living in North America today.

The Black Hills of South Dakota play an important role in Sioux spiritual life.

IMPORTANT ANIMALS
CHAPTER 3

Horses and bison have been huge parts of the Sioux way of life for centuries. Horses were introduced to the Sioux in the 1700s, after the Sioux acquired them from other peoples who had, in turn, acquired them from the Spanish. Horses changed life for the Sioux dramatically. These animals made travel easier. Horses could move much more weight more quickly than dogs. Entire villages of people and all their goods could be moved easily and quickly.

The Sioux, especially the Lakotas, used horses to make hunting bison easier. Bison provided for nearly every Sioux need—not just for food, but for clothing and shelter as well. The Sioux fashioned bison horns into spoons and large bones into weapons. A successful bison hunt was an occasion for a great feast. One bison, weighing a ton (0.9 mt) or more, provided more fresh meat than could be eaten at one time. The remaining meat was cut into strips and dried in the sun, making jerky that would last a long time.

Because horses made hunting bison easier, the Sioux had more food than ever before. This allowed more Sioux children to grow into adulthood. The Sioux grew in both population and power as they improved their horseback riding skills.

The Lakotas were especially good riders. Because of this, they also became especially good at hunting bison.

TENSIONS ON THE RISE
CHAPTER 4

The Sioux didn't have much contact with settlers of European descent until U.S. leaders began to expand the nation westward. Then, thousands of settlers began to pass through or near Sioux lands as they moved west. In 1851, the Sioux signed a treaty with the U.S. government that opened their lands to settlers traveling west on the Oregon Trail.

In 1854, however, a dispute over a cow that had wandered away from a wagon train sparked violence between Lakotas and members of the U.S. Army. The leader of the U.S. soldiers was killed in the violence, along with all 28 of his men. The next year, the army struck back by destroying a Lakota village.

The Dakotas also fought against settlers who were taking their lands in Minnesota. After an uprising in which they killed hundreds of settlers, the U.S. government hanged 38 Dakotas. This is the largest mass execution in U.S. history.

Tensions rose even higher between the Sioux and the U.S. military when gold was discovered in the heart of Lakota country. Even the sacred Black Hills were soon overrun by gold seekers after it was confirmed that gold was found on this part of Sioux land.

Crazy Horse and Red Cloud were famous Lakota warriors who helped their people fight against the U.S. military in the 1860s. The left photo shown here may be a photo of Crazy Horse, although there's some doubt. The right photo shows Red Cloud. Both men led their people in important ways for many years as they fought to protect the Lakota way of life.

FROM VICTORY TO DEFEAT

CHAPTER 5

The discovery of gold in the Black Hills led to the most **definitive** defeat of the U.S. military by Native Americans. On June 25, 1876, the Sioux and their Cheyenne allies took up arms against Lieutenant Colonel George Armstrong Custer and his troops near the Little Bighorn River in what's now Montana. The Battle of the Little Bighorn resulted in the deaths of Custer and all his men. For this reason, the battle is also known as Custer's Last Stand.

Sitting Bull (below) was a Lakota chief who helped defeat Custer and his troops at the Battle of the Little Bighorn.

After this stunning victory, however, the United States sent out large numbers of troops and forced all the Sioux and Cheyenne people to surrender within a year. Meanwhile, hunters—with the help of the U.S. Army—were killing bison herds in huge numbers. Without the animal they depended on, the Sioux lost much of their way of life and were forced to accept life on **reservations**, mostly in North Dakota and South Dakota.

One Sioux leader, Sitting Bull, led his followers to Canada to avoid capture by the U.S. military. However, exhaustion and a lack of food forced him to surrender in 1881. Even after his surrender, he still fought against government efforts to force the Sioux to give up their culture and values.

THE GHOST DANCE AND WOUNDED KNEE

CHAPTER 6

The **transition** to reservation life was hard on the Sioux people. Their sadness led them to embrace a new religion that swept through the reservations in 1890. The Ghost Dance religion was founded on the idea that, if the Indians embraced the Ghost Dance, the bison would return, along with all the Native Americans who'd died. In addition, all the white people would disappear.

Sitting Bull embraced the new religion, which made some U.S. leaders worried. He was ordered to stay away from Ghost Dance **rituals** in the Black Hills. He said that he was going to go

Ghost Dance

against that order, but he was killed by reservation police during an attempt to arrest him.

In December 1890, a Sioux leader named Big Foot—who didn't follow the Ghost Dance religion—tried to call for peace before another war broke out with the United States. However, the army was unaware that Big Foot was trying to encourage peace. They surrounded his band, and a gun went off as they attempted to take the Sioux's weapons. The army then went on the attack. Over 250 Sioux men, women, and children died in this **massacre** at Wounded Knee. Following this event, the Sioux no longer tried to fight against reservation life.

Shown here is the site of the Wounded Knee Massacre in South Dakota. It's now a U.S. National Historic Landmark.

RESERVATION LIFE

CHAPTER 7

Reservation life continued to be difficult for the Sioux people throughout the nineteenth and twentieth centuries. Americans in the late nineteenth century believed there was no place in their society for Native American culture. The reservation system was designed to force Native Americans, including the Sioux, to abandon their traditions, religions, and languages. The government attempted to force them to adopt white values in a process called **acculturation**.

In the early days of the reservation system, Native American children were taken far from their homes and sent to boarding schools, where they were forced to learn English. Today, Sioux living on reservations have more freedom to practice their traditions and religion.

The traditional Sioux government was no longer allowed. Poverty, unemployment, poor health, and high death rates were common on reservations.

By the 1970s, Native Americans from around the country were determined to change the conditions on reservations. A number of young Sioux became members of the American Indian Movement (AIM) and traveled to Washington, D.C., in what became known as the "Trail of Broken Treaties." They took control of the headquarters of the Bureau of Indian Affairs.

By drawing attention to the problems facing Native Americans in such a public way, the Sioux and other members of AIM forced the government to take action. Native Americans were allowed once again to practice their own religions. This helped the Sioux and other nations recover the culture that was once taken from them.

SIOUX LEADERSHIP

CHAPTER 8

The traditional Sioux government isn't recognized by the U.S. government, but large Sioux families often have their own informal government with their own leaders. These leaders act in a way that reflects early forms of Sioux government.

In the early days of the Sioux people, their basic unit of government was the *tiyospaye*. Each *tiyospaye* consisted of about 30 or more households of related families who spent the entire year together.

Each *tiyospaye* had a headman who achieved and kept his position by virtue of his character. Traditional Sioux leaders were known for their wisdom, courage, and compassion, as well as their ability to gain spiritual guidance from dreams and visions. However, a leader could lose their power by failing to live up to these high standards. The most respected headmen were admitted into male societies called *nacas*. The most important of these was called the *Naca Omincia*, which had the power to make war and peace.

Other Sioux leaders of both the past and present include medicine men and women. They're healers who are respected for their ability to cure illnesses and heal people spiritually. Medicine men and women are also known as wise leaders among their people.

A medicine man is also known to the Sioux people as a *wicasa wakan*. Medicine men and medicine women still play important roles in modern Sioux life.

RELIGIOUS TRADITIONS

CHAPTER 9

Religion plays a big part in modern Sioux life, and it helps the Sioux feel connected to their history as a nation. Traditionally, the Sioux believe in a Creator, which is sometimes called the Great Mystery. They believe the Great Mystery is present in all things on Earth, including rocks, trees, animals, water, and wind. They seek guidance from the Creator in dreams and visions, which medicine men interpret.

For the Sioux, Bear Butte in the Black Hills is a place for fasting and praying in order to seek a vision to guide one's life. However, Bear Butte is currently controlled by the U.S. government. The Sioux must pay fees to U.S. park rangers to enter this land.

Despite this, the Sioux still hold on to their religious traditions and ceremonies. Their most important religious ceremony, which is called the Sun Dance, is held every summer. Ceremonies such as the Sun Dance help the Sioux cleanse their spirits and renew their vows to work for the welfare of their community. Helping the whole community is important to the Sioux. Sharing with others is valued. The Sioux also believe in living in harmony with nature and other people.

Shown here is Bear Butte in South Dakota, which is sacred ground for Sioux who practice their people's traditional religious beliefs.

SIOUX ARTISTS AND WRITERS

CHAPTER 10

Sioux artists and writers have worked hard in the past and are working hard in the present to bring the Sioux way of life into the spotlight. Oscar Howe, who lived from 1915 to 1984, was a Sioux who lived on the Crow Creek Reservation and became one of the best-known Indian artists in North America. Kevin Locke is a famous Sioux flute player and hoop dancer.

Floyd Red Crow Westerman was a Sioux musician who lived from 1936 to 2007. He was

Floyd Red Crow Westerman

a country music singer who later became an actor. He appeared in many movies, such as *Dances with Wolves*, and on television shows, such as *The X-Files*.

Virginia Driving Hawk Sneve is a Sioux who's famous for writing children's books. She won the 1992 North American Indian Prose Award. In addition to her children's books, she's written history books for adults such as *Completing the Circle*, which traces the histories of the women in her family. Vine Deloria Jr. was a well-known Sioux author and scholar who died in 2005. There are many other Sioux authors who publish poetry or fiction. Their work is an important part of college courses in Native American literature.

Vine Deloria Jr., shown here, was also a lawyer and a teacher. He taught at many colleges and universities in the western United States.

A DIVIDED PEOPLE

CHAPTER 11

Although reservation life for the Sioux is better now than it once was, the Sioux people are still faced with hardships. Many Sioux have moved to large cities, but about half the Sioux continue to live on reservations throughout Minnesota, Montana, North Dakota, and South Dakota.

The Sioux people are still divided between wanting to follow their old ways and adopting nonnative values. In the 1970s, this divide led to violence on the Pine Ridge

The occupation of Wounded Knee in 1973 brought attention to the problems facing not just the Sioux but all Native Americans.

Reservation, and nearly 100 traditional Sioux people were killed. In 1973, members of AIM occupied the church at Wounded Knee, which is located on this reservation. They held it as the center of an independent Indian nation for 71 days. While this struggle within the Sioux nation continues today, it's no longer marked by the violence that brought attention to the Pine Ridge Reservation during the 1970s.

The Sioux who live on reservations today often work for U.S. government agencies and programs. Many others work in cattle ranching and mining. There aren't many industrial jobs on Sioux reservations because they're located far from manufacturing centers. Poverty is still a concern on Sioux reservations, and Sioux schools suffer from a lack of funding.

Wounded Knee occupation, 1973

FIGHTING FOR THE BLACK HILLS

CHAPTER 12

The Sioux have faced many struggles as a people, and there's one fight they've never given up: the fight for the Black Hills. The Sioux continue to push the U.S. government to return their most sacred land to them.

In proceedings before the U.S. Indian Claims Commission, the Sioux won a decision that the Black Hills had been taken from them illegally. In 1980, however, the U.S. Supreme Court ruled that the Sioux were only entitled to money and not the land itself. The Sioux have refused to take the money and continue to demand that the Black Hills be returned to them.

In 2007, a group of Sioux **activists** led by Russell Means formed the Lakota Freedom Delegation. They declared all the traditional homelands of the Lakota people independent from the United States. However, this group's actions haven't been backed by Tribal Councils on the Sioux reservations.

The Sioux continue to fight for their sacred land to this day. They haven't given up trying to convince Congress to pass legislation to return the Black Hills to them. They've even spoken to representatives from the **United Nations** about their cause.

PLEASE DO NOT DISTURB PRAYER BUNDLES AND PRAYER CLOTHS

The Sioux have been fighting for the Black Hills for centuries, and they won't rest until their sacred land has been returned to them.

PAST, PRESENT, AND FUTURE

CHAPTER 13

Life for the Sioux may not be easy, but they continue to fight for what's important to them, especially their traditional way of life. They may not have much money, but other things matter more to them. They value a rich and rewarding family life with their relatives and the entire community more than trying to make money. The Sioux people's sense of respect for others and nature has helped them remember what's important through war, poverty, and attempts to rob them of their culture.

The Sioux people's understanding of what is and isn't important is a measure of their success at surviving an era when their culture was almost wiped out forever. Instead of losing hope, they worked hard to preserve their values and traditions. Though they still face many problems, they've produced many capable leaders who are working to solve those problems. They've also produced many great artists and writers who are finding ways to keep their culture alive and to share that culture with the whole world. The Sioux people are an important part of Native American history, and they're ready to be an important part of the future of Native Americans in the United States, too.

This member of the Sioux nation is speaking at the site of a memorial dedicated to the Sioux people who fought at the Battle of the Little Bighorn. This memorial is one way the Sioux people's past is being honored in the present.

GLOSSARY

acculturation: The process of trying to change the culture of a person or group of people by having them adopt the traits of another culture.

activist: Someone who acts strongly in support of or against an issue.

culture: The beliefs and ways of life of a certain group of people.

definitive: Not able to be argued about or changed; the best of its kind.

descent: Referring to a person's ancestors.

dialect: A form of language spoken in a certain area that uses some of its own words, grammar, and pronunciations.

massacre: The violent killing of many people who are often helpless or unresisting.

reservation: Land set aside by the government for a specific Native American group or groups to live on.

ritual: A religious ceremony, especially one consisting of a series of actions performed in a certain order.

transition: A passage from one state, stage, or place to another.

unique: Special or different from anything else.

United Nations: An organization formed in 1945 to promote international cooperation.

FOR MORE INFORMATION

BOOKS

Benoit, Peter, and Kevin Cunningham. *The Sioux*. New York, NY: Children's Press, 2011.

Rzeczkowski, Frank. *The Lakota Sioux*. New York, NY: Chelsea House, 2011.

Sanford, William R. *Hunkpapa Lakota Chief Sitting Bull*. Berkeley Heights, NJ: Enslow Publishers, Inc., 2013.

WEBSITES

Due to the changing nature of Internet links, PowerKids Press has developed an online list of websites related to the subject of this book. This site is updated regularly. Please use this link to access the list: www.powerkidslinks.com/sona/sioux

INDEX